Mirroring Your Vision™

*Become Self-Aware, Intentional,
and Mindful When Leading Your LIFE*

Janet J. Sawyer, EdD

Published by
WSA Publishing
301 E 57th Street, 4th fl
New York, NY 10022

Copyright © 2019 by Janet J. Sawyer

All rights reserved. No part of this book may be reproduced or transmitted in any form or by in any means, electronic or mechanical, including photocopying, recording, or by any information storage and retrieval system, without the written permission of the Publisher, except where permitted by law.

Manufactured in the United States of America, or in the United Kingdom when distributed elsewhere.

Sawyer, Janet J.
    Mirroring Your Vision: Become Self-Aware, Intentional and Mindful When Leading Your LIFE
    ISBN: 978-1-948181-61-7

Cover design by: Joe Potter
Cover photo by: Nikkie Achartz, SNAP Savvy Strategies
Interior design: Claudia Volkman

Mirroring Your Vision™

There is a thinking stuff from which all things are made, and which, in its original state, permeates, penetrates, and fills the interspaces of the universe. A thought, in this substance, produces the thing that is imagined by the thought. Man can form things in his thought, and, by impressing his thought upon formless substance, can cause the thing he thinks about to be created.

                Wallace D. Wattles (2009)
                The Science of Getting Rich, p.21

Table of Contents

Introduction   1

Step 1: Commit to Creating the Life of Your Dreams   3

Step 2: Begin the Journey with a Song   5

Step 3: Imagine the Results You Want   11

Step 4: Think BIG!   17

Step 5: Commit to the Power of 48   29

Step 6: Review the Journey   35

Step 7: Manifest Using the Magic of 68 Seconds   37

Step 8: Where Do We Go from Here?   47

Five Virtues to Support You   51

Helpful Resources   54

About the Author   55

MIRRORING YOUR VISION™

INTRODUCTION

*"The universe isn't giving you a plan, and it's waiting for yours.
If you ask for it, the universe will bring it to you."*
—Kyle Gray

If someone stopped you on the street and asked you, "What do you want the gift and purpose for your life to be?" how would you respond? Are your answers written down?

Three years ago, I remember asking myself, "What if I could come up with a way to teach people how to unlock what they really want from their mind and heart?" And so I decided to design a **Mirroring Your Vision**™ experience.

My name is Dr. Janet "JJ" Sawyer, an **educator, leadership expert/coach, personality styles specialist, published author, and professional speaker.** For the past three years, I have been coaching clients to create the life they want and fulfill their dreams. When coaching, I use an intensely growth- and goal-oriented process for entrepreneurs, students, parent groups, sales teams, and company business leaders when creating the vision for their business and personal lives.

Through the process I use, clients discover their power by becoming Self-Aware, Intentional, and Mindful when becoming clear about how they want to live and work. Having been involved with personal and professional growth and development for over forty-five years, I am thrilled that I have been able to turn my passion into a business that coaches in a way that provides the results my clients are looking for living their lives the way they want.

MIRRORING YOUR VISION™

The ***Mirroring Your Vision*™** process has eight steps:

1. Commit to Creating a Life of YOUR Dreams.
2. Begin the Journey with a Song.
3. Imagine the Results You Want.
4. Think Big.
5. Commit to the **Power of 48.**
6. Review Your Journey.
7. Manifest with the **Magic of 68.**
8. Where Do We Go from Here?

Join me and learn and experience the eight-step process for identifying your gift and purpose for your life by completing this **Mirroring Your Vision™** workbook. Are you ready to explore what you want? Are you ready to see yourself in your vision? Well then, let's get started!

MIRRORING YOUR VISION™

Step 1: Commit to Creating the Life of YOUR Dreams

*"It's only when you make the process your goal
that the big dream can follow."*
—Oprah

First, I would like to thank you for taking this first step by choosing to participate in **Mirroring Your Vision™**. Before you go through the exercises, I'm going to ask you to commit to doing the work throughout this **Mirroring Your Vision™** Workbook, making a decision to follow the process from the beginning to the end.

Materials Needed and Time Required for Completing the Process:

- A pencil and pen
- An 8"x11" sheet of heavy aluminum
- Two colored permanent marker pens
- Internet access to YouTube for listening to a song
- A timing device for measuring time in seconds
- A mirror of your choice (minimum size 8.5"x11" inches) for the 48-hour step

You will need to set aside at least two hours of uninterrupted time to complete this workbook.

Commitment means going for your goals and dreams wholeheartedly with passion. I invite you to not hold back and act with commitment in choosing

MIRRORING YOUR VISION™

to complete the **Mirroring Your Vision™** process. Read the statements below and commit to growing and learning by putting your initials by each statement.

I commit to . . .

. . . giving myself permission to learn and grow.
. . . setting aside two hours of uninterrupted time.
. . . completing the exercises at the end of each chapter.
. . . reflecting on what I am learning about myself.
. . . sharing what I am learning with someone I trust.

Signed _____   Date _____

Now, let's do the WORK!

MIRRORING YOUR VISION™

Step 2: Begin the Journey with a Song

"The two most important days in your life are the day you were born and the day you find out WHY."
—Mark Twain

When I was studying to be a life coach, I listened to many coaching sessions, some of those being with Tony Robbins, Jack Canfield, Patrice Washington, and Kevin Trudeau. As I listened, I heard this from each one of them over and over: "Most people don't even know what they want. It seems that people go through the day without any thought of what they want. They get up, drink coffee, get dressed, take a shower, and just go through their daily routine."

When I heard, "People do not know what they want," I remember thinking, *That can't be true.* So I decided to find out, and here's my true story. I decided to find six people of different ages and ask them what they wanted in life. I went walking around my community and the shopping center across the street from where I live, and I found four women and two men, with their ages ranging from twenty-three to seventy-five.

The first person was a man in his seventies. We had a short conversation, and then I asked, "If you could do anything you wanted, what would you want to do?" He said, "Well, I don't want any bills. I don't want to have to work." I responded by saying, "Oh, I can understand what you're saying, but I didn't ask you what you didn't want. I asked you, 'What DO you want?'" He stopped and took a pause and said, "Oh, um, that's a great question."

Next I began talking to a young woman in her twenties who worked in a small woman's boutique. I asked her the same question. "If you could do anything you wanted, what would you want to do?" To my surprise she said, "Well, I don't want to work here. I don't want to work forty hours a week." And I said,

"Oh, I can understand what you're saying, but I didn't ask you what you didn't want. I asked you, 'What DO you want?'" She then paused and said, "Hmm . . . I've never been asked that."

As I continued, the same thing happened over and over again. Out of the six people I spoke to, not one person could tell me what they wanted in their lives. They all told me what they didn't want.

I thought that day, *What if I could come up with a way to teach people how to unlock in their minds what they really want?*

I decided to design the **Mirroring Your Vision™** Workshop and Workbook. It includes the eight-step process I had been using for the past four years. In the beginning of creating the process, I started with making a vision board by cutting and gluing pictures from magazines on to a poster board. From there I glued these pictures on to a mirror instead of the poster board so I could see myself in the vision I was creating. I then decided to write exactly what I wanted on my mirror, instead of using the pictures, so when I read it, I would be able to see myself in my vision.

This is when **Mirroring Your Vision™** was born. Are you ready to explore what you want? Are you ready to see yourself in your vision? Well, then . . . let's get going with a song!

MIRRORING YOUR VISION™

"If I Were Brave"

DOWNLOAD JANA STANFIELD—IF I WERE BRAVE.MP3

Before we start, I want you to either download by clicking the above link or go to YouTube and listen to the song, **"If I Were Brave"** by Jana Stansfield. As you listen to the song, write phrases and words that speak to you.

What I Like About the Song

In 2005 after retiring from the educational field, I attended a business conference with three hundred people so I could figure out what I was going to do next with my life. Jana Stansfield, an inspirational speaker that shares her message through songs, was the keynote presenter. She walked on stage with a guitar and started to sing "If I Were Brave." When Jana sang this song that day, she looked directly at me. The lyrics spoke to me in such a way that they deeply touched my heart, and I started to think, *What would I do today if I were brave?*

The song kept playing over and over in my mind. From that day on, and even today, anytime I hear the words in my mind, "What would I do today if I were brave?" they propel me forward to the next level of what I want to achieve in my life.

What words or phrases spoke to you?

_____

_____

_____

MIRRORING YOUR VISION™

Get excited to start your journey!

As you read each step and work through the exercises in the ***Mirroring Your Vision*™** workbook, you will experience a process in which you will have an opportunity to identify what you would do today if you were brave. You will learn how to write goals that will excite and scare you at the same time, and you'll experience the Power of 48 hours and the Magic of 68 seconds.

Some of you will need to call on the **virtue of courage** within you to transform your fear into determination. It will take embracing life fully without holding back and doing what must be done even when it is difficult.

"What would I do today if I were brave?"

I would do something BRAVE!

MIRRORING YOUR VISION™

Develop a Winner's Mindset

Watch the following video on YouTube and write what speaks to you. Think about what you learned while going through the process of **Mirroring Your Vision**.

WINNER'S MINDSET
Tony Robbins, Jim Rohn, Les Brown

https://youtu.be/6_5ZfO1stO0

As you listened to Tony Robbins, Jim Rohn, and Les Brown, what spoke to you? Write a few thoughts that you feel will help you while going through the Mirroring Your Vision process.

_____

_____

_____

_____

_____

_____

MIRRORING YOUR VISION™

Step 3: Imagine the Results You Want

*"Set a goal to achieve something that is so big, so exhilarating
that it excites you and scares you at the same time."*
—Bob Proctor

Creativity Is the Power of Imagination

The process of imagination begins with the ability to first connect to your inspiration. *It's the process of being mentally stimulated to do or feel something, especially to do something creative* (according to Siri). As we grow older, some of us we lose the ability to imagine due to our life experiences, for whatever reason. What do you love to do? What do you really want? What you really want comes from your fantasies, and these originate through the effective use of your imagination.

I invite you to sit quietly before you begin this process of imagination and connect to your inspiration and creativity, as this never diminishes as we grow older. The more you use your creativity, the more it will develop within you and will improve your imagination.

So, what is *imagination*? According to Siri, its definition is "the ability of the mind to be creative or resourceful; A part of the mind that imagines things."

Blocks to Unleashing Your Imagination

For some of us, imagining what we do want in life can be difficult, and for others it comes naturally. What gets in the way of using our imagination is having a fixed mindset rather than a growth mindset. Some of you might be asking, "What's the difference?"

We all have beliefs about our own abilities and potential. These beliefs are part of our mindset, which is so powerful that it can fuel our behavior and interfere with being able to imagine. Mindset helps us to interpret our experiences and future possibilities. We can choose to look at what we are imagining in a way that makes us feel we can achieve it and be happy. This is a growth mindset. Or we can imagine in a way that makes us feel frustrated and think that we will never have what we want; this is a fixed mindset.

You see, people with a fixed mindset believe they are stuck with the way things are. They might even think that imagining is difficult. Or that they are not worthy enough to have what they really want in life. For example, some of you might imagine you would like to own a house but think to yourself that you can't afford it. It's not about what you can afford, however; it's about imagining what you desire, what you yearn for in life, or a wish that you have had for many years.

If you are having a challenge with unleashing your imagination because your fixed mindset is getting in the way, learn to debate with yourself by saying: "Every day I let my imagination soar to new heights!" You might want to even start saying to yourself, "My imagination is the most powerful tool I possess!"

In this next exercise I invite you to let your imagination soar!

MIRRORING YOUR VISION™

EXERCISE: Unleash Your Imagination

Using the lines below provided, write down four things you want personally and two things you want professionally. Then put them in order of importance. What would you want first, second, and so on?

Example:
Personal   *Professional*

✔ House   1. House   ✔ A Teacher   1. An Author

✔ Pets   2. Car   ✔ An Author   1. A Teacher

✔ Car   3. Travel

✔ Travel   4. Pets

The above is my personal example. Now it's your turn. Yours could include family, relationships, career, or retirement. Let yourself relax and let your imagination wander.

NOTE: In this step many people tend to put money first; however, money comes last in the overall process of Mirroring Your Vision™. It's not about the money. It's about what we do in life to make the lives we touch better.

MIRRORING YOUR VISION™

My Personal and Professional Wants

What I want personally is: (Write one word next to each of the checkmarks. Then choosing in order of importance, write what you want personally next to each number.)

✔ _____   1. _____

✔ _____   2. _____

✔ _____   3. _____

✔ _____   4. _____

What I want professionally is: (Write one word next to each of the check marks. Then choosing in order of importance, write what you want professionally next to each number.)

✔ _____   1. _____

✔ _____   2. _____

MIRRORING YOUR VISION™

Develop Your Imagination

Watch the following video on YouTube and write what speaks to you. Think about what you learned while going through the process of *Mirroring Your Vision*.

Develop Your Imagination
Proctor Gallagher Institute

https://www.youtube.com/watch?v=CkL9eRJlnic

As you listened to this video, what spoke to you? Write a few thoughts that you feel will help you while going through the Mirroring Your Vision process.

_____

_____

_____

_____

_____

_____

MIRRORING YOUR VISION™

MIRRORING YOUR VISION™

Step 4: Think BIG!

*"Think little goals and expect little achievements.
Think big goals and win big success."*
—David Joseph Schwartz

Thinking big is about imagining the possibilities and giving yourself permission to dream. It is about being able to visualize what you can achieve on an audacious scale with no limits on your thinking. It is about being open-minded, positive, creative, and seeing opportunity in the big picture. It is the view inside you.

Visualizing Is a Very Large Part of Manifesting Your Desires.

It is important to form a picture in your mind of what you want. A good way to start seeing what you want in your mind's eye is to think of everything and anything you would have if money was not an object and you could not fail. This will get your imagination going with all sorts of ideas. Roll with the momentum and let your mind keep thinking of things that make you feel good, things you would like to have in your life.

On the next pages there are some reflection questions to get you thinking.

MIRRORING YOUR VISION™

What makes you happy?

_____

_____

_____

_____

_____

What are you really passionate about?

_____

_____

_____

_____

_____

MIRRORING YOUR VISION™

How do you want to be remembered?

_____

_____

_____

_____

_____

When you're feeling empowered and inspired, what do you want to contribute to the world?

_____

_____

_____

_____

_____

MIRRORING YOUR VISION™

What do you want to experience in your life if time and money weren't an issue?

_____

_____

_____

_____

_____

What does success look like to you?

_____

_____

_____

_____

_____

MIRRORING YOUR VISION™

As you imagine the things you want, start pretending you have already received them. Feel how good that feels. Stay in the feeling as long as you can. If you can start to do this every day, you will exercise your imagination. When unwanted images enter your mind, shift your thinking back to a more positive growth mindset. Do it consciously, and it will become easier over time.

PERSONAL Want—Goals and Statement

On Page 16 you put your **PERSONAL wants** in order of importance. Choose the one you put first when completing this section.

Example:
In my **PERSONAL** wants list, I chose a house as my Number 1 want.

GOALS: I want my house to have:
- Two bedrooms and two bathrooms
- 1,450 square feet
- A gated community where they have plenty of activities that bring the community members together on a monthly basis
- To be across the street from a shopping area because I do not drive
- To be close to the ocean

GOAL STATEMENT: I am so happy, thankful, and grateful now that I am living in my house that has two bedrooms and 1,450 square feet. It is in a gated community that has monthly activities where I get to connect with community members once a month. I live right across the street from a shopping center that has everything I need, and I am close to the ocean.

Now it's your turn!

MIRRORING YOUR VISION™

EXERCISE: PERSONAL Want—Goals and Statement

1. Write down your number one **PERSONAL** Want.
2. Think about and write down the goals for creating your ideal GOAL statement. It should be a GOAL statement that makes you excited and scared all at the same time.
3. Then fill in the ideal GOAL sentence and statement.

1. My number one PERSONAL Want is:

I want _____

_____

2. My goals related to my PERSONAL want are:

_____

_____

_____

3. Write your PERSONAL Want using the above goals to create one GOAL Statement.

Start the sentence with the following words:
I am so happy, thankful, and grateful now that I am _____

_____

_____

MIRRORING YOUR VISION™

PROFESSIONAL Want—Goals and Statement

Now let's do the same exercise that we did for your **PERSONAL Want**, for working on your **PROFESSIONAL Want**. What impact will you make on this planet? In other words, what is your passion, purpose, or gift to the world? For identifying your professional want goals, we will use the word *why*. On page 8 you put your **PROFESSIONAL Wants** in order of importance.

Choose the one you put first when completing this section. For example, in my **PROFESSIONAL** Want, I chose to be an author.

Here is my EXAMPLE:

My number one **PROFESSIONAL Want** is to be the author of a book.

Why? I want to teach others how to define their purpose/gifts in life. Everyone is born with a purpose/gift, and I want to help others to uncover and become aware of theirs.

Why? Sometimes people get influenced by what others want them to do. Their purpose/gifts get buried inside of them. Once people know their purpose/gifts, they can be more intentional about taking responsibility for how they are developing themselves.

GOAL STATEMENT: I am so happy, thankful, and grateful now that I am on the bestsellers list, selling my book all over the world and making people more aware of their purpose/gifts! **I am so happy, thankful, and grateful now that I am earning** $550,000 a year.

Now it's your turn!

MIRRORING YOUR VISION™

EXERCISE: PROFESSIONAL Want—Goals and Statement

1. Write down your number one **PROFESSIONAL Want**.
2. Think about and write down the goals for creating your ideal GOAL statement. It should be a GOAL statement that makes you excited and scared all at the same time.
3. Fill in the ideal goal sentence and statement.

1. My number one PROFESSIONAL Want is: _____

I want _____

_____

2. The Whys related to my PROFESSIONAL want are:

Why? _____

Why? _____

3. Write your PROFESSIONAL Want GOAL statement using the above "Whys."

Start the sentence with the following words:
I am so happy, thankful, and grateful now that I am _____

_____

_____

MIRRORING YOUR VISION™

Now that you have all this money and you're able to be and have what you want, how did you earn your money? How much money are you earning? **Think BIG!**

4. I am so happy, thankful, and grateful now that I am earning $ _____ a year.

MIRRORING YOUR VISION™

Combining Your PERSONAL and PROFESSIONAL Wants

Go back to the pages where you wrote your **PERSONAL and PROFESSIONAL Wants**. You are going to put them both on this page. When writing them, write as if you already have what you desire.

PERSONAL

I am so happy, thankful, and grateful now that I am _____

_____

_____

PROFESSIONAL

I am so happy, thankful, and grateful now that I am _____

_____

_____

Starting Your Mirroring Process

Aluminum Foil

Now that you have written your personal and professional wants, it is time to first write them on an 8.5"x11" sheet of aluminum foil. Take your colored markers and write your goals on to your foil sheet as if they have already happened. You might like to either do a mind map or a written list. (Refer to the chart on page 31.)

MIRRORING YOUR VISION™

Commit to Achieving Your Dreams

Watch the following video on YouTube and write what speaks to you. Think about what you learned while going through the process of **Mirroring Your Vision**.

Make Commitments to Achieve Your Dreams
Kevin Trudeau

https://youtu.be/bJmsTwZDUPg

As you listened to Kevin Trudeau, what spoke to you? Write a few thoughts that you feel will help you while going through the **Mirroring Your Vision** process.

_____

_____

_____

_____

_____

_____

MIRRORING YOUR VISION™

MIRRORING YOUR VISION™

Step 5: Commit to the Power of 48

"Right now, no matter where you are, you are a single choice away from a new beginning."
—Oprah Winfrey

The one thing I found during my life is that people are always very open to learning. Across the country and internationally, many of you are going to school, reading books, attending conferences, seminars, going to workshops, all in the pursuit of gaining more knowledge in order to better yourselves by improving your skills. Right?

My question is, "Are you taking what you have learned and applying it in your everyday life?" Does it really happen? If you are one of those people that have attended conferences, workshops and classes, met wonderful people, made connections, and learned some great strategies, how have you applied what you have learned when you have gotten home and gone back to work, school, or just your daily life?

Do you do exactly what you've always done? You enjoyed the experience, met some wonderful people, but often very little changes in your life. You go back to business as usual. Does this sound like you?

One thing I've learned over the years of doing personal development is that all the information is great! But it is impossible to apply all of it, so the information goes on the shelf or becomes a wonderful memory, never to be thought of or looked at again.

So, what do you do? How do you hold yourself accountable when it comes to applying what you've learned? Where do you start?

What I've learned over the years is the importance of paying attention to the aha moments. Have you ever heard of the aha moment?

Aha moments are when you hear something that makes you go, "Ah, that makes sense to me," or "Ha, I never thought about that." This is the secret I believe will help you apply what you've learned when personally developing yourself.

The way you identify your aha moments is to think about the two or three things that touched you during a conference, workshop, or even when you're reading and learning from a professional development book. I believe these moments are the only things you're meant to apply to your life right now ... within the next 48 hours.

I call it the **Power of 48**. The power comes from making a commitment to implement one or two things you've learned and will apply within a 48-hour period. When making those 48-hour steps, they must be very small steps—the smaller the step, the bigger the gain. Here are a few examples to get you started.

Exercise: 48-Hour Action Steps

When I first began creating this process, I learned that seeing myself inside my vision, writing it on a mirror, was so much more powerful than just reading it on a piece of paper. Now that you have identified your personal and professional goal statements, it is time to complete Step 5 by starting the process of **Mirroring Your Vision™** so that you can see yourself within it. There are two parts to this mirroring process. First, though, here is an example of the statements I wrote on my mirror:

Your first 48-hour action step is to complete the Mirroring Your Vision ™ process. Purchase or use a mirror from your home, and transfer what you wrote on your aluminum foil to your mirror. Use your markers when writing your statements. See example on the next page.

MIRRORING YOUR VISION™

Mirror of My Vision:

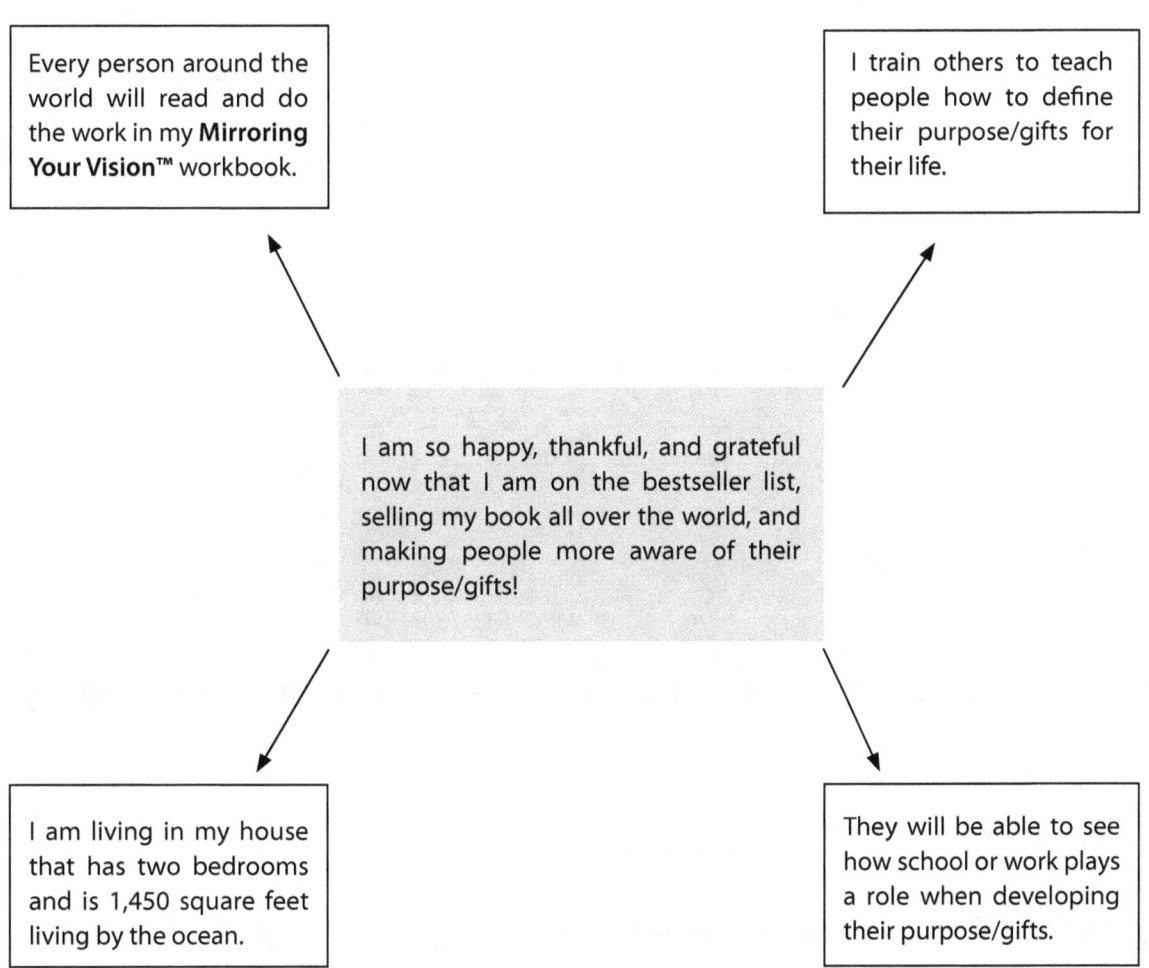

I am so happy, thankful, and grateful now that I am earning $550,000 a year.

MIRRORING YOUR VISION™

Write the **48-hour action step you can commit to** in the next **48 hours** to move toward your goals. Remember, the smaller the step, the bigger the gain.

_____

_____

_____

_____

_____

Now, ask yourself two questions. Write "yes" next to each statement if you believe it:

1. "Am I able to do it?" _____

2. "Am I willing to do whatever is required?" _____

MIRRORING YOUR VISION™

Step into Your Purpose

Watch the following video on YouTube and write what speaks to you. Think about what you learned while going through the process of **Mirroring Your Vision**.

Stepping into Your Purpose
Lisa Nichols

https://www.youtube.com/watch?v=YQnpM0Nx7O0

As you listened to this video, what spoke to you? Write a few thoughts that you feel will help you while going through the **Mirroring Your Vision** process.

_____

_____

_____

_____

_____

_____

MIRRORING YOUR VISION™

MIRRORING YOUR VISION™

Step 6 – Review the Journey

*"Writing is not just a process of creation.
It is also a process of self-discovery."*
—Cristina Istrati

Step 6 is all about giving yourself an opportunity to see where you have come from in your **Mirroring Your Vision**™ process, which has turned into a self-reflection journey. The mind map on the following page will give you a chance to read and review each of the steps you completed.

MIRRORING YOUR VISION™

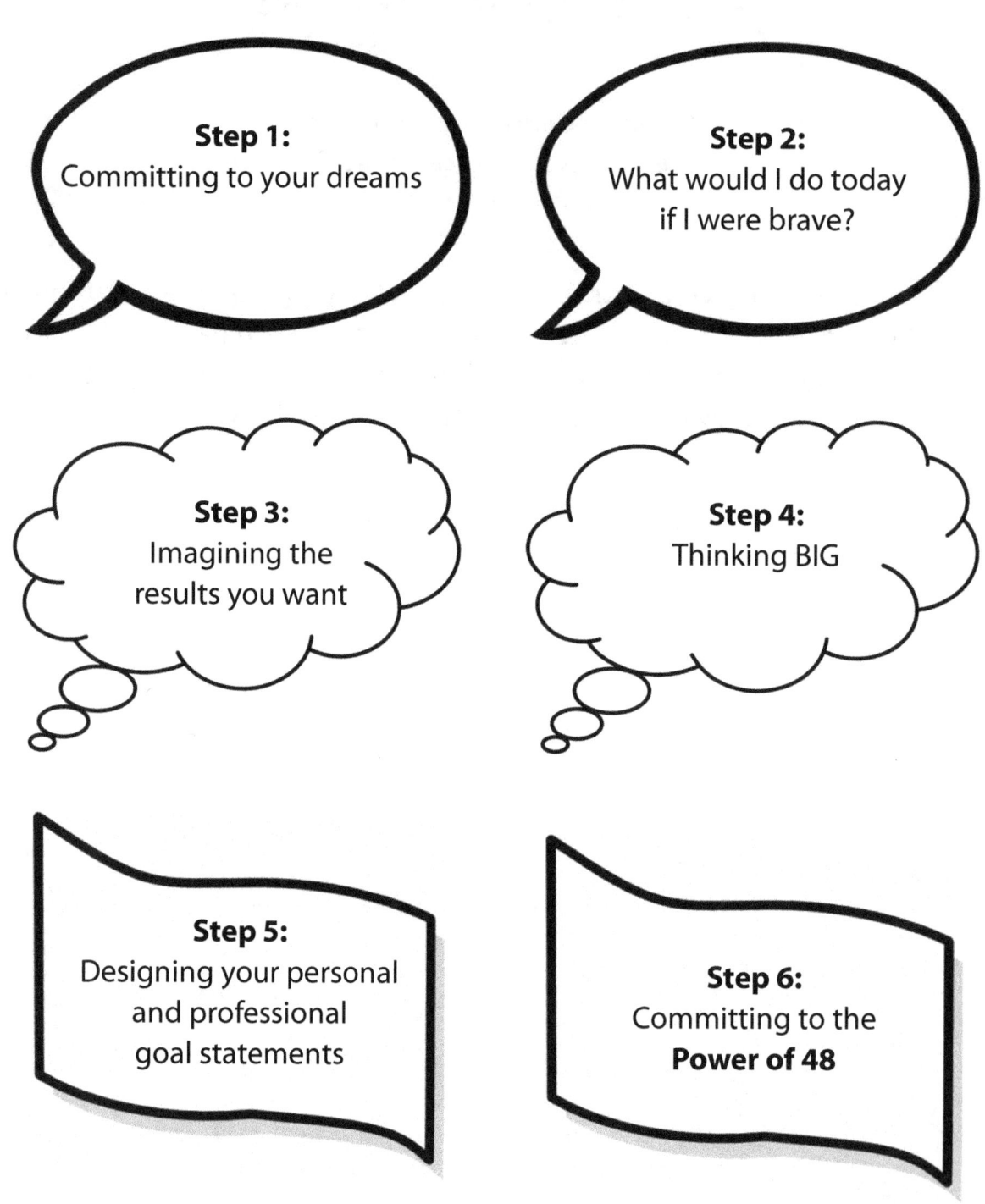

MIRRORING YOUR VISION™

Step 7: Manifest Using the Magic of 68 Seconds

*"Hold a thought for just 17 seconds and the Law of Attraction kicks in.
Hold a thought for 68 seconds and things move;
manifestation has begun."*
—Abraham-Hicks, *"Ask and It Is Given"*

Now that you have reviewed steps 1 to 6, you are now ready to move onto the most exciting step of all! In Step 7 you will learn the Magic of 68 Seconds. This step teaches how to apply the law of attraction in your life.

A friend of mine, Debbie MacEachen, says that we are all vibrational beings. So, what does that mean? She says we and everything else on this planet emit our own unique vibrations out to the Universe every day. In fact, our brains are actually transmitters and receivers of vibration or energy. There are particles flowing from our brain out to the Universe. Thoughts create things!

Debbie goes on to say that it's so important to be aware of what you're thinking. Focused attention on a thought or feeling (negative or positive) for more than 17 seconds is long enough to attract like thoughts—thoughts that prove you "right"; thoughts that agree with the original thought or feeling.

It is not necessary to police your thoughts at all times, but beware of sending out vibrations that are not in line with your thoughts and desires. When you do, try to shift the vibration of the thought a bit higher to avoid giving attention to the unwanted thoughts. Be the master of your mind.

When a thought is held—with feeling and belief that the desired result has already occurred—for at least 68 seconds, the Universe has no recourse except to bring back, through the Law of Attraction, things, events, and people with that same vibration.

The Law of Attraction says that what we put out to the Universe is returned to us. This has been stated in many ways: karma; what goes around comes around; as you sow, so shall you reap. It is one of the Laws of the Universe. The vibration that you send out attracts people, events, and circumstances of the same vibration. In this way, each of us has the power to manifest our goals and desires by paying attention to the thoughts we think or the words we speak.

Think about what you want. Talk about what you want. Imagine what you want—use your five senses. Don't spend time on things you don't want. Remember when I told you about my little research when I spoke to those four women and two men? I asked them what they wanted, and all of their answers were about what they didn't want.

You don't want to fall into that trap. Start today by becoming aware of what you are thinking. When you find yourself thinking about what you don't want, shift your thoughts back to what you do want!

Change that fixed mindset into a growth mindset by becoming aware of your thoughts and learning to debate with yourself daily.

MIRRORING YOUR VISION™

How Does the Law of Attraction Work?

Think about one of the goals or desires you wrote on your mirror. Does the thought of it make you smile? Does it make you feel scared and excited at the same time? Great! This is a goal that resonates with you! It's something that excites you, something you can believe in.

Once you are in a high vibration, focus on the feelings of having what you desire. Use all five senses! Feel, smell, taste, hear, and see the future just the way you want it. Use your imagination!

We all have the power to manifest our goals and desires. Using the Law of Attraction, we create momentum by focusing on the feelings of having the results. With at least 68 seconds of focused attention on your goals and desires, you will send your thoughts out to the Universe. The Law of Attraction then brings it back to you.

Set your timer or use your ManifesTimer (manifestime.com). Maintain focused attention on the goals and desires you wrote down on your mirror until the time or sand runs out. Do this every morning and every night when creating what you want in your life. Remember this process is about becoming self-aware, intentional, and mindful when creating the life you want for yourself.

For more information on 68-second manifesting or to purchase a ManifesTimer, go to manifestime.com or the ManifesTime page on Facebook.

MIRRORING YOUR VISION™

MIRRORING YOUR VISION™

Using these seven steps, now go back and look at the second-most important personal and professional wants you identified. On the following pages repeat the exercises you did on pages 18 through 21, this time with your number two goals.

MIRRORING YOUR VISION™

EXERCISE: PERSONAL Want—Goals and Statement

1. Write down your number two **PERSONAL** Want.
2. Think about and write down the goals for creating your ideal GOAL statement. It should be a GOAL statement that makes you excited and scared all at the same time.
3. Then fill in the ideal GOAL sentence and statement.

1. My number two PERSONAL Want is:

I want _____

_____

2. My goals related to my PERSONAL want are:

_____

_____

_____

3. Write your PERSONAL Want using the above goals to create one GOAL Statement.

Start the sentence with the following words:

I am so happy, thankful, and grateful now that I am

_____

_____

MIRRORING YOUR VISION™

EXERCISE: PROFESSIONAL Want—Goals and Statement

1. Write down your number two **PROFESSIONAL Want**.
2. Think about and write down the goals for creating your ideal GOAL statement. It should be a GOAL statement that makes you excited and scared all at the same time.
3. Fill in the ideal goal sentence and statement.

1. My number two PROFESSIONAL Want is: _____

I want _____

_____

2. The Whys related to my PROFESSIONAL want are:

Why? _____

Why? _____

3. Write your PROFESSIONAL Want GOAL statement using the above "Whys."
Start the sentence with the following words:
I am so happy, thankful, and grateful now that I am _____

_____

_____

MIRRORING YOUR VISION™

Now that you have all this money and you're able to be and have what you want, how did you earn your money? How much money are you earning? **Think BIG!**

4. I am so happy, thankful, and grateful now that I am earning $_____ a year.

Starting Your Mirroring Process (see page 30)

Aluminum Foil

Now that you have written your personal and professional wants, it is time to first write them on an 8.5"x11" sheet of aluminum foil. Take your colored markers and write your goals on to your foil sheet as if they have already happened. You might like to either do a mind map or a written list. (Refer to the chart on page 31.)

Write the **48-hour action step you can commit to** in the next **48 hours** to move toward your goals. Remember, the smaller the step, the bigger the gain.

_____

_____

_____

_____

_____

MIRRORING YOUR VISION™

Now, ask yourself two questions. Write "yes" next to each statement if you believe it:

1. "Am I able to do it?" _____

2. "Am I willing to do whatever is required?" _____

Manifesting

We all have the power to manifest our goals and desires. Using the Law of Attraction, we create momentum by focusing on the feelings of having the results. With at least 68 seconds of focused attention on your goals and desires, you will send your thoughts out to the Universe. The Law of Attraction then brings it back to you.

Set your timer or use your ManifesTimer (manifestime.com). Maintain focused attention on the goals and desires you wrote down on your mirror until the time or sand runs out. Do this every morning and every night when creating what you want in your life. Remember this process is about becoming self-aware, intentional, and mindful when creating the life you want for yourself.

MIRRORING YOUR VISION™

Apply Oprah's Secret to Success

Watch the following video on YouTube and write what speaks to you. Think about what you learned while going through the process of *Mirroring Your Vision*.

Oprah's Powerful Secret to Success Using the Law of Attraction

Oprah Winfrey

https://youtu.be/bJmsTwZDUPg

As you listened to Oprah, what spoke to you? Write a few thoughts that you feel will help you while going through the *Mirroring Your Vision* process.

_____

_____

_____

_____

_____

_____

MIRRORING YOUR VISION™

Step 8—Where Do We Go from Here?

*"The very least you can do in your life is to figure out what you hope for.
And the most you can do is live inside that hope."*
—Barbara Kingsolver

You can use the process of Mirroring Your Vision™ in many different areas of your life to create and manifest what you desire. Some of the areas my clients have focused on manifesting are:

- Ideal relationships
- Physical fitness and health
- Ideal career
- Travel
- Growing a business
- Parenting
- Making a difference to humanity
- Ideal hobby or recreational activity
- Ideal car, boat, caravan, or mobile home
- Ideal vacation

These are just some examples of the areas people can focus on. I encourage you to open your mind to the many possibilities for creating the life of your dreams. On the next page, there is space for you to journal about this. Remember, think BIG!

MIRRORING YOUR VISION™

MIRRORING YOUR VISION™

Practice . . . Practice . . . Practice . . .

Every morning and every night, stand in front of your mirror, set your timer for 68 seconds, and follow the process of the Magic of 68. We all have the power to manifest our goals and desires. Using the Law of Attraction, we create momentum by focusing on the feelings of having the results. With at least 68 seconds of focused attention on your goals and desires, you will send your thoughts out to the Universe and the Law of Attraction then brings it back to you. Maintain focused attention on the goals and desires you wrote down on your mirror until the time or sand runs out, and experience your life the way that you design it!

Testimonials

Here are some of my clients' experiences of going through the Mirroring Your Vision ™ process.

Laura (mother) said: I wanted to learn how to identify and focus my thinking in order to turn goals into reality. Identifying goals and going through the process of seeing what I will achieve made my goals real and attainable. Not only was the workshop beneficial for me, but my daughters, ages seven and eleven, benefited from going through the process. I wanted them to attend the workshop to teach them how to identify and think about their goals, with a process that they could use their whole life. The girls both enjoyed going through the steps of the workshop; they discovered that writing can help you set your goals, and seeing what you want can make it happen.

Erin (author and musician) said: I was fortunate enough to have a Mirroring Your Vision™ session with Dr. JJ Sawyer earlier this year, and the process was truly life-changing (a phrase I don't use lightly!). Dr. JJ helped me crystalize the perfect vision for what I wanted my future to look like, both personally and professionally. Within a few days of my session, I started noticing a difference in my outlook on life and also in the way I viewed my values and myself. Since our session, every element of my life has improved, and I feel not just happy, but grounded, safe, and secure in my path.

Paula (media show host) said: Clarity was the biggest gift I received from the Mirroring Your Vision™ process. Dr. Sawyer was extremely skilled at guiding me through the clutter of my confusion and getting me to a place where I felt that my goals and dreams for my life were clear and possible. In fact, within 48 hours of doing the process, doors started opening to help me attain those goals. It was very powerful.

Sandra (entrepreneur) said: The biggest gift I got from participating in the Mirroring Your Vision™ process with Dr. JJ Sawyer was to finally get that I didn't have to be perfect and always get things right to achieve my vision and goals in life and in my business. I also now have a way to daily work at a deeper metaphysical level on achieving my dream, through applying the Power of 48 and the Magic of 68 processes. Thank you so much, JJ—what a gift you have given me!

MIRRORING YOUR VISION™

Five Virtues to Support You

When attracting your personal or professional vision I have identified five Virtues that will support you to attract the goals you have designed during your **Mirroring Your Vision™** process. Some people find that a number of Virtues come naturally to them and have been developed from a very young age. For example, the Virtue of Friendliness is when you reach out to others in a warm and caring way. When you are practicing Friendliness, it makes others feel welcomed. Some of us are naturally very friendly, and some of us are not. We can all be friendly though and often it's the situation we find ourselves in that has us choose to be friendly.

The following five Virtues will support you when working toward your dreams:

- Courage
- Commitment
- Perseverance
- Faith
- Trust

Courage is embracing life fully without holding back, doing what must be done even when it's difficult or risky.

Commitment is caring deeply about a goal. Once you discern a direction, you go for it. You don't hold back, second-guess the direction or hesitate to act on it fully.

MIRRORING YOUR VISION™

Perseverance is having the will to carry on. Once you discern your true direction, you stay the course for however long it takes, regardless of obstacles that arise.

Faith is a relationship of trust. You are confident your life has a purpose. Faith is the wind in the sails of your dreams.

Trust is positive expectation that all will be well. You move confidently with the flow of life, gathering strength from adversity.

Read the Virtue definitions provided and practice demonstrating them each and everyday. By this I mean demonstrate the Virtue behaviors, mindset, attitude, language and intensity of energy. For example, in what situations would you need to practice Courage, Commitment, Perseverance, Faith and Trust? How would you need to be? What would you need to say?

Here is a link to a virtues app you might find helpful:

    https://itunes.apple.com/us/app/virtues-reflection-cards/id326312834?mt=8

I recommend that you choose one Virtue at a time to practice and develop while reading your Mirror each and everyday. Once you feel you have developed this Virtue, then move on to another one. Before you know it, you will be able to naturally demonstrate each one when working toward any goals you might have.

MIRRORING YOUR VISION™

Congratulations!

You have started the process of
Manifesting YOUR DREAMS and DESIRES!

MIRRORING YOUR VISION™

Helpful Resources

Podcasts

Attract Anything in 17 Seconds: The Real Secret of the Law of Attraction—Robert Zink

Manifesting My Own Destiny—Oprah Winfrey Show

Books

Key to Living the Law of Attraction by Jack Canfield (Audiobook)

The Law of Attraction by Micheal Losier

The Secrets Behind "The Secret": What You Need to Know About the Law of Attraction and Dream Manifestation by Daniel Marques

How to Manifest Anything: A Simplified Guide for Using the Law of Attraction to Live an Awesome Life by Beau Norton

About the Author

Janet J. Sawyer, EdD, is a lifelong learner, education professional, and published author. She has served as a leadership consultant for a nationally recognized education research company; an adjunct professor of leadership for two universities; a middle school principal in which she was awarded Principal of Year for the state of Colorado; and an elementary and middle school teacher—her first passion. She is also certified in the PeopleSmart DISC Interpretation Method with PeopleSmart World.

www.ingramcontent.com/pod-product-compliance
Lightning Source LLC
Chambersburg PA
CBHW081732100526
44591CB00016B/2592